How to Write an Investment Policy Statement

BY ROCCO DIBRUNO
AIFA® CIMA®
ACCREDITED INVESTMENT FIDUCIARY ANALYST

Marketplace Books
Glenelg, Maryland

WILEY

TRA

SEC

Titles in the FP Books Trade Secrets Series

The Life Insurance Handbook
By Louis S. Shuntich, JD, LLM

How to Write an Investment Policy Statement
By Rocco DiBruno

How to Build, Protect, and Maintain Your 401(k) Plan
Strategies & Tactics
By Dale Rogers & Craig Rogers

Asset Allocation Essentials
Simple Steps to Winning Portfolios
By Michael C. Thomsett

The Long-Term Care Planning Guide
Practical Steps for Making Difficult Decisions
By Don Korn

Understanding ERISA
A Compact Guide to the Landmark Act
By Ken Ziesenheim

Best Practices for Investment Committees
By Rocco DiBruno

Wiley Trading Series

Founded in 1807, John Wiley & Sons is the oldest independent publishing company in the United States. With offices in North America, Europe, Australia and Asia, Wiley is globally committed to developing and marketing print and electronic products and services for our customers' professional and personal knowledge and understanding.

The Wiley Trading series features books by traders who have survived the market's ever changing temperament and have prospered—some by reinventing systems, others by getting back to basics. Whether a novice trader, professional or somewhere in-between, these books will provide the advice and strategies needed to prosper today and well into the future.

For a list of available titles, visit our Web site at www.WileyFinance .com.

Library of Congress Cataloging-in-Publication Data:

ISBN 9781118679531 (Paperback)
ISBN 9781118680216 (ePDF)
ISBN 9781118680124 (ePub)

Printed in the United States of America

10 9 8 7 6 5 4 3 2

Contents

SECTION ONE: Why Plan Sponsors and All Fiduciaries Need a Formal Process for Writing Their Investment Policy Statement

SECTION TWO : How to Get Started and Steps to Formalize the Process

SECTION THREE: The Template IPS

Chapter 10

Conclusion

Glossary 69

Appendix: The Firm Profile 77

About the Author 79

Foreword

The preparation and maintenance of the Investment Policy Statement (IPS) is the most critical function a fiduciary performs, for a well-written IPS becomes the narrative that defines how all of the investment-related responsibilities will be prudently managed. —Don Trone

This statement is particularly relevant to defined-contribution plans — and yes, even participant-directed plans. Unfortunately, for three key reasons, a large number of retirement plans either do not have an IPS, lack a formal process for drafting one, or have prepared a document that is of little value. First, during the strong bull-market days, many companies saw little need to implement a consistent process, because few complaints were filed by customers. Plan sponsors also found the "prudent man" criteria — that defines for advisors the practices that constitute a prudent investment process — so vague and poorly defined that they could not easily develop guidelines that would assure them compliance. And finally, while ERISA (the Employee Retirement Income and Security Act) stipulates that a well-articulated, documented procedure for investment selection and ongoing investment evaluation is a fiduciary *obligation*, there has been little regulatory pressure for enforcement.

However, the current investment climate has changed dramatically, and there is even talk that having a formal Investment Policy Statement will become a legal requirement. In fact, ERISA implies that the financial advisor is advised and cautioned to discuss fiduciary-related matters with qualified legal counsel, and in the event of registered representatives, with their broker-dealer's compliance department.

A financial advisor plays a pivotal role in assisting plan sponsors in the management of investment decisions, particularly the preparation and maintenance of a formal IPS.[1] By helping plan sponsors with the management of their IPS, they are, in effect, providing the structure and evidence that a clear investment process and methodology are being followed, which fulfills their fiduciary obligation outlined in ERISA.

Now this compact new strategy guide provides advisors and their fiduciary clients with a useful tool that will help them comply with their ERISA-directed requirement. DiBruno furnishes an easy-to-follow framework to properly utilize and realize the benefits of an Investment Policy Statement. He outlines the essential contents of a well-written IPS based on the fiduciary practices that have been identified by the Foundation for Fiduciary Studies.[2] Sections include:

- Defining the specific investment strategy.
- Defining the duties and responsibilities of all parties involved.
- Defining diversification guidelines.
- Defining due diligence criteria for selecting investment options.
- Defining monitoring criteria for investment options and service vendors.
- Defining procedures for controlling and accounting for investment expenses.

For more than 30 years, successful investors and sophisticated investment committees have used the IPS as their "business plan" for managing critical investment decisions. The objective of this guide is to impart their knowledge and to provide you with confidence that you are servicing your clients with the highest standards of care and

---

[1]The Foundation for Fiduciary Studies has recently released, in cooperation with the AICPA, the fiduciary handbook, *Prudent Investment Practices*. Copies of the handbook can be obtained from Thornburg Investment Management at www.Thornburg.com, or through the Foundation: www.ffstudies.org.

[2]ERISA (Employee Retirement and Income Security Act) in Sec. 404(a)(1)(B).

protection from personal liability, and staying in compliance with all federal regulations and industry standard practices.

And, whether you follow the guidelines delineated in DiBruno's guide, or those developed by your own team, I urge you to impress upon all of your colleagues and fiduciary clients the importance of preparing and maintaining a standard IPS.

Donald B. Trone
Strategic Ethos, CEO (Chief Ethos Officer)

SECTION ONE
Why Plan Sponsors and All Fiduciaries Need a Formal Process for Writing Their Investment Policy Statement

Chapter 1

ERISA AND THE CHALLENGE OF FIDUCIARY RESPONSIBILITY

The landmark Employee Retirement Income Security Act of 1974, or ERISA, protects the assets of millions of Americans so that funds placed in retirement plans during their working lives will be there when they retire. This act is a federal law that sets minimum standards for retirement plans in private industry.

ERISA requires retirement plans to provide participants with information about the plan, including important information about plan features and funding. It also requires accountability of plan fiduciaries. ERISA generally defines a fiduciary as anyone who exercises discretionary authority or control over a plan's management or assets within the plan, including anyone who provides investment advice to the plan. Fiduciaries who do not follow the principles of conduct may be held responsible for restoring losses to the plan. Courts may take whatever action is appropriate.

Writing an Investment Policy

The U.S. Department of Labor enforces Title I of the Employee Retirement Income Security Act (ERISA), which, in part, establishes participants' rights and fiduciaries' duties. This guide addresses one crucial fiduciary duty in particular—the writing of an investment policy—and gives the reader an example of how to structure a policy, how to write the policy, and why it's so critical.

> **Anyone who is a trustee, sponsor, or who otherwise exercises any authority or control over any type of employee-benefit plan is a *fiduciary*.**

And, while the contents of ERISA are immense, it is our intention to help plan sponsors, trustees, and advisors fulfill their fiduciary obligations by offering a simple step-by-step process. This process will show plan sponsors, and their advisors, how to design an investment policy that will aid in the selection of plan participants' investment options; how to write an IPS; and how to establish a thoughtful monitoring process that will ensure the process is being prudently executed.

Employer-sponsored profit sharing, 401(k), and other defined-contribution plans were designed to attract, retain, and motivate employees, while also accumulating and preserving individual retirement funds for workers. In order to accomplish these human-resource goals, someone, or some group, has to be responsible, and with that responsibility comes a legal obligation. We call these responsible people *fiduciaries*. Anyone who is a trustee, sponsor, or who otherwise exercises any authority or control over any type of employee-benefit plan is a fiduciary.

What Is a Fiduciary?

The ERISA definition of a fiduciary[3] is as follows:

- Person(s) who exercises any discretionary authority or control in management or administration of the plan or its assets.
- Person(s) who renders investment advice for a fee or other compensation (may or may not include brokers).
- Those named as plan sponsors, trustees, investment advisors (who are paid a fee), and plan administrators.

Even though there are an estimated 6 million fiduciaries in the United States today responsible for managing trillions of dollars of

---

[3] Center for Fiduciary Studies.

investable assets, a large percentage of these fiduciaries may not be aware of just what their fiduciary duties include. How could that be? Well, for nearly 20 years we have had strong investment markets and enjoyed a period when most investors made money and few complaints were registered. Consequently, there was little need to scrutinize the list of fiduciary obligations. But things are very different today. Yesterday's fiduciary may have been *aware* of Section 404(c) "safe harbor" regulations that outline the specific actions plan sponsors can take to limit their personal liability—but had little motivation to put them in place.

Fiduciary Liability

Today's knowledgeable fiduciaries are not just required to—but motivated to—stay abreast of the regulations and follow them to the letter. They understand that the rules to which they must adhere are governed by the U.S. Department of Labor, the Internal Revenue Service, and the Pension Benefit Guaranty Corporation. And, with the current volatility in the financial markets, coupled with corporate malfeasance seen at numerous companies, and the historical concentrations of company stock in 401(k) plans, participants who experience losses are upset and looking for someone to blame. Plan sponsors are a logical target. The Center for Fiduciary Studies estimates that there were over 15,000 ERISA-related actions (civil actions and arbitration cases) brought against plan fiduciaries in 2002—representing an 11.7 percent increase over the prior year.

> **The critical first step in building a structure for ERISA conformity is to write and implement an investment policy statement (IPS). This single action is crucial to ensuring that you, your company, and/or your committee are in compliance and protecting your personal liability.**

There are steps a plan sponsor (fiduciary) can—and must—take to protect themselves from personal liability and assist in compliance with their responsibilities. The critical first step in building a structure for ERISA conformity, and the one we focus on in this book, is to write and implement an investment policy statement (IPS). This single action is crucial to ensuring that you, your company, and/or your committee are in compliance and protecting your personal liability.

Developing an IPS for your defined-contribution plan is a key component of fulfilling a plan sponsor's fiduciary responsibilities. Current estimates indicate that less than 50 percent of all defined-contribution plans have an IPS, due primarily to a lack of understanding about why one is important, and how to prepare it. This book will help you structure one, if you don't already have one. Or, if you do have one, it will provide you with a simple reference for reviewing your existing plan to make sure it encompasses all of the key issues of compliance.

PLEASE NOTE: While it's my hope that this book will be of value to plan sponsors, plan trustees, and investment advisors, it does not offer legal advice, legal opinions, or investment advice. It was written strictly to help fiduciaries with the common language needed to create a clear and understandable IPS.

Chapter 2

YOUR FIDUCIARY RESPONSIBILITIES AND LIABILITIES UNDER ERISA

You may be the owner of a small company, a retirement plan director or an attorney who has been named as a trustee on behalf of your company's participant-directed defined-contribution plan. As trustee, you are a named fiduciary. In addition to named fiduciaries, under ERISA there are also "deemed fiduciaries," which include any person(s) who exercises any discretionary authority or control in management or administration of the plan or its assets. Once you understand that you are a fiduciary, the next step is to understand how to comply with your fiduciary responsibilities under ERISA.

Five Fiduciary Responsibilities

Every fiduciary, regardless of plan size, has the following five responsibilities:

1. **Duty of Loyalty** — To act to ensure that the plan assets are used exclusively for the benefit of the plan participants and beneficiaries; avoid conflicts of interest.

2. **Duty to Diversify** — To ensure that the plan offers a diversified investment menu that allows participants to minimize the risk of long-term losses. If the plan is not diversified, the fiduciary bears the burden of proof as to why it was not prudent to diversify.

3. **Incur Only Reasonable Costs** — Know what you are paying for in total plan expenses and how these costs compare to the market for reasonableness. You do not need to have the least expensive plan, but you do need to know what you are paying for and how those costs compare to the market.

4. **Monitor Investments** — Implement an ongoing program for evaluating your plan's investment managers for consistency of style, performance against appropriate benchmarks, and significant changes in management.

5. **Avoid Prohibited Transactions** — A fiduciary shall not cause the plan to engage in a transaction if he/she knows that the transaction constitutes a direct or indirect:

   • Sale, exchange, or leasing of property between the plan and a party in interest; or

   • Lending money or other extension of credit between the plan and a party in interest; or

   • Furnishing of goods, services, or facilities between the plan and a party in interest; or

   • Transfer to, or use by, or for the benefit of, a party in interest; and/or

   • Acquisition and retention of employer securities, or employer real property, in violation of ERISA statutes.

Fiduciary's Personal Liability

In addition to knowing what a fiduciary's responsibilities are, a fiduciary must also be keenly aware that she/he has personal liability (which includes home, personal assets, and business assets) for restoring any lost profits resulting from a violation of fiduciary responsibility under ERISA. In fact, ERISA Section 409A states: "Any person who is a fiduciary with respect to a plan, who breaches any of the responsibilities, obligations, or duties imposed upon fiduciaries by this title shall be personally liable to make good to such plan any profits of such fiduciary which have been made through use of assets of the plan by the fiduciary, and shall be subject to such other equitable or remedial relief as the court may deem appropriate, including removal of such fiduciary."

A Fiduciary's Primary Role Is to Manage the Process

With this personal liability incumbent upon them, it is extremely important that fiduciaries understand that compliance with ERISA is primarily a procedural process. Compliance with your fiduciary responsibilities does not require that you have the best-performing investment choices available to your participants all the time, with the lowest cost. A fiduciary's primary role is to manage the process. That is, a fiduciary's responsibility is to provide the essential management of the investment process, without which the other components of the investment plan cannot be defined, implemented, or evaluated.[4] Good management of the investment process will reduce most concerns about fiduciary liability. The environment has become one of "It's not whether you win or lose the game, it's *how* you play the game."[5]

Given that fiduciaries are responsible for managing the process, the next challenge is defining the investment process. Developing a formal investment process, and documenting that process will assist fiduciaries to prudently manage their defined-contribution plan assets and will help them substantially reduce their fiduciary liability.[6]

---

[4]Center for Fiduciary Studies.

[5]Ibid.

[6]The Profit Sharing/401(k) Council of America (PSCA) is a nonprofit association advocating increased retirement security through profit-sharing, 401(k), and related defined-contribution programs.

Chapter 3

WHAT IS AN INVESTMENT POLICY STATEMENT AND WHAT ARE THE BENEFITS?

A n IPS is a written document outlining the process for a plan sponsor's investment-related decision making. Its purpose is to describe, formally, how investment decisions are related to a plan's goals and objectives, as well as to document the plan's strategic vision for plan investment. A written IPS can also provide a framework for participant communication and education.

> **An IPS is a written document outlining the process for a plan sponsor's investment-related decision making.**

Risk Management

Fiduciaries who have neither described the investment procedures required by ERISA in a written IPS nor documented their implementation may render themselves vulnerable to legal action from disgruntled plan participants or the U.S. Department of Labor. A significant benefit of writing an IPS is that it forces fiduciaries to comply with the procedural mandates of ERISA. It provides a very important paper trail you may need if problems develop in the plan's future.

> **An IPS's purpose is to describe, formally, how investment decisions are related to a plan's goals and objectives, as well as document the plan's strategic vision for plan investment. A written IPS can also provide a framework for participant communication and education.**

Further, a well-constructed IPS provides evidence that a clear process and methodology exist for selecting and monitoring plan investments. In fact, in the process of a plan audit, the Department of Labor will routinely ask to see a plan's investment policy within the initial audit notification and information request letter.

It is virtually impossible to document what the investment policy *is* without having a formal Investment Policy Statement.

Monitor Investments

Section 402(b) of ERISA states: "Every employee benefit plan shall provide a procedure for establishing and carrying out a funding policy and method consistent with the objectives of the plan. . . ." In other words, ERISA stipulates that a well-articulated, documented procedure for investment selection and ongoing investment evaluation is a plan sponsor's fiduciary obligation. Without a written description of procedures affecting plan investment decision making, the plan sponsor has an obligation to provide evidence linking plan objectives and the proper exercise of fiduciary responsibility for every plan investment-related decision, which is typically difficult to create for every individual. The existence of an IPS provides evidence of a prudent investment decision-making process and, in doing so, can serve a risk-management role as the first line of defense against potential fiduciary liability.

In addition to legal and regulatory reasons for adoption of an IPS, the ever-increasing number and variety of defined-contribution investment offerings is encouraging many plan sponsors to consider developing an IPS. An expansion of core investment offerings (including a variety of investment styles and disciplines, and self-directed brokerage products), is available on today's defined-contribution investment landscape. This expansion makes a consistent road map to navigate these choices even more important. Furthermore, in creating an IPS, the plan sponsor can help those responsible for investment decisions now, and in the future, avoid the temptation of following short-term "fads" in the financial markets.

Summary

In summary, implementing an IPS has practical advantages for the plan sponsor, because it:

- Helps clarify the plan's investment-related goals and objectives.
- Provides a framework for evaluating investment performance.
- Aids in clear communication of plan investment policy to participants.
- Supports continuity in decision making as plan fiduciaries change.
- Protects the sponsor from inadvertently making capricious or arbitrary decisions. Helps the sponsor manage pressure for change generated by participants, vendors, or the media.

Chapter 4

UTILIZE THE "SAFE HARBOR" PROVISIONS PROVIDED BY ERISA

A fiduciary's primary responsibility is to manage the investment process. ERISA provides sponsors of participant-directed defined-contribution plans two methods for reducing their fiduciary liability. The first method is to hire "prudent experts" to execute the investment process; and the second is to have a plan that is compliant with Section 404(c) as described next.

Prudent Experts

ERISA encourages plan sponsors and other fiduciaries to hire "prudent experts" to execute the investment process developed by the fiduciary, and provides a "safe harbor" from certain liabilities when prudent experts are used and properly monitored. Fiduciaries who take it upon themselves to execute the process by investing funds on behalf of the plan participants are taking undue fiduciary liability that can, and should, be avoided.

Five Recognized "Safe Harbor" Rules

For plans where the investment decisions are being made by an investment committee and/or an investment advisor, there are five generally recognized "safe harbor" rules that must be met when using prudent experts to help alleviate fiduciary liability, including:

1. **Investment Decisions**—Use prudent experts to make the investment decisions, which includes selecting the actual bonds and stocks. A prudent expert is defined as: *a regulated financial services entity, including banks, insurance companies, registered investment advisors, and registered investment companies (mutual funds).*

2. **Defined Due-Diligence Process**—Select the prudent expert utilizing a well-defined, consistently applied due-diligence process.

3. **Discretionary Control**—Give the prudent expert discretion over the assets.

4. **Co-Fiduciary Acknowledgment**—Have the prudent expert acknowledge their co-fiduciary status in writing.

5. **Monitor**—Check the prudent expert's activity in a well-defined, consistent manner to ensure compliance with agreed-upon tasks.

Chapter 5

COMPLYING WITH ERISA SECTION 404(c)

Fiduciaries are able to limit their liability for actual investment decisions made by plan participants in participant-directed 401(k) plans, if they are fully compliant with 404(c). While the plan sponsor has oversight responsibility for all aspects of the 401(k) plan, (including writing an IPS, selecting plan investment options, and monitoring expenses), most plan sponsors will want to have each plan participant responsible for his or her investment selections among the options offered. A plan sponsor not in compliance with ERISA Section 404(c) might be liable for losses resulting from the investment selections and allocations chosen by the participants.

Section 404(c) provides specific actions that plan sponsors can take to limit their liability for participant's investment decisions. They are:

1. **Notify**—Plan participants are to be notified in writing that the plan will constitute a 404(c) plan, including a statement that the fiduciaries of the plan may be relieved of certain liabilities.

2. **Identify**—Participants must be notified in writing as to who the plan fiduciary is (name, address, and phone number) and how to request information from the fiduciary. A log of participant information requests and how/when they were fulfilled should be maintained.

3. **Diversify**—Offer a broad menu of diversified investment options to allow participants to minimize the risk of large losses. The average number of investment options per plan today is about 10 although ERISA mandates only three.

4. **Educate** — Provide plan participants with sufficient education about the different investment options so each participant may make an informed decision appropriate to his/her circumstances. Participant education should include:

- Information on investment managers.
- A copy of the prospectus for each investment option before or after the initial investment.
- General description of the investment objectives and the risk/return characteristics for each investment option.
- Information on the fees and expenses associated with each investment option.
- A listing of securities held by each investment option.
- Portfolio statistics (e.g., alpha, Sharpe ratio, and standard deviation) for each investment option.

5. **Opportunity to Change** — Allow participants the opportunity to change their investment strategy/allocation at least quarterly. Make sure the participants have been clearly informed about how to make investment instructions and to whom.

6. **Company Stock Policy** — Include a policy that relates to the use of company stock in the plan, if applicable.

IMPORTANT — When preparing an IPS for a defined-contribution plan intending to comply with 404(c), it is required that the IPS include an explicit statement that the plan intends to be 404(c) compliant and written notification of this intent must be provided to each plan participant. Remaining in compliance with 404(c) is a process that must be managed on an ongoing basis.

SECTION TWO
How to Get Started and Steps to Formalize the Process

Chapter 6

ASSEMBLING THE DOCUMENTATION

Prior to beginning the writing of the IPS, it is imperative that a fiduciary take the time to understand the applicable laws affecting the plan as well as the particular needs of the plan. You begin to develop this level of understanding by gathering and thoroughly analyzing the relevant documents that pertain to the defined-contribution 401(k) plan for which the IPS is being developed.

Included in this list of relevant documents are:

- Trust documents, including amendments.
- Summary plan description and all plan documents.
- Written minutes of the Committee meetings.
- Service agreements with all vendors (managers, custodian, consultants, attorneys, etc.).
- Investment performance reports from money managers, custodians, and consultants.
- Enrollment activity reports.
- Participant education material.
- Loan activity reports and procedure manuals.
- IRS Form 5500 and all related schedules.
- Independent audit report, if applicable.

As you conduct your review of these documents, it is important to determine whether the existing plan documents include a formal process for making investment-related decisions, whether the trust documents identify the trustees and named fiduciaries, whether the trust documents delegate investment decisions to others, and finally, whether the trust documents restrict or prohibit the use of select asset classes.

Understanding the idiosyncrasies of the trust is key to developing a thoughtful IPS that will meet the needs of the trust and withstand the test of time without requiring constant modifications and updates (unless needs and circumstances change).

Important—Now that these plan documents have been gathered, you have the beginnings of a fiduciary audit file. This fiduciary audit file and the finished IPS should be filed together and be easily accessible for review in the event of an audit for compliance.

Chapter 7

STEPS TO FORMALIZE
THE PROCESS

The following are the specific actions and required steps necessary when assembling an IPS.

STEP 1: Decide on Plan Goals, Objectives, and Strategies

The trustee must give reasonably careful consideration to both the formulation and the implementation of an investment strategy, with investments to be selected and reviewed in a manner reasonably appropriate to that strategy. A trustee's investment and management decisions must be evaluated as part of an overall investment strategy designed to meet pre-established plan objectives. Specific goals should be established in terms of investment performance with appropriate benchmarks identified to monitor results.

STEP 2: Decide on Strategy for Managing Risk

Modern fiduciary law now recognizes the Nobel Prize-winning work of Harry Markowitz on risk management, which has since become known as *Modern Portfolio Theory*. This groundbreaking concept is based on a disarmingly simple concept: An investor's desire is not simply to maximize the return of a portfolio; rather it is to maximize the portfolio return while simultaneously minimizing the portfolio's risk. Risk management, rather than risk avoidance, has become the standard.

Low levels of risk may be appropriate in some trust settings but inappropriate in others. It is the trustee's task to invest at a risk that is suitable to the purpose of the trust. Today's investment strategy is not about the avoidance of risk by trustees but for their *prudent management of risk*. Risk management takes account of all hazards that may follow from inflation, volatility of price and yield, lack of liquidity, and so forth.

Markowitz pioneered the concept of blending investments together in a manner that lowered overall volatility of the total portfolio. Even though individual investments within a portfolio might be considered to be "risky" or volatile, Markowitz found that if you blend together two investments, even so-called "risky" investments, the overall risk of the portfolio or the overall volatility may be significantly reduced.

His theory has evolved into the popular concept of an "Efficient Portfolio," which relies on blending together baskets of different investments specifically for the purpose of controlling the volatility risk of the whole, or total, portfolio. The overall returns that the whole portfolio earns could, thereby, be enhanced or preserved through the balance, thereby adding value to the portfolio itself. And it is incumbent upon the modern-day fiduciary to recognize each client's risk tolerance and manage each portfolio so that it conforms to this standard.

STEP 3: Determine the Risk Tolerance of the Plan

Investment fiduciaries must not only consider the purposes, terms, distribution requirements, and other circumstances of the trust, they must also consider the risk tolerance and risk attributes *for each asset inside the plan*. Thus, an investment fiduciary must be able to not only manage risk, he/she must have an understanding of how to evaluate the risk profile for each asset class inside the plan.

Risk management requires that as much careful attention be given to the particular trust's risk profile as is to its volatility attributes. The trustee can recommend investing in anything that plays an appropriate role in achieving the risk/return objectives of the trust. Returns correlate strongly with risk, but risk standards vary greatly with the financial and other circumstances of the trust. Therefore, it is the trustee's task to invest at a risk that is suitable to the purpose of the trust.

STEP 4: Set Forth Guidelines for Asset Classes

The investment policy document should provide clear guidelines for asset classes to be considered. Basic asset classifications might begin with cash equivalents, bonds, asset-backed securities, real estate, and corporate stocks, with both debt and equity categories further divided by their general risk-reward or income/growth characteristics, by the domestic, foreign, tax-exempt, or other characteristics of the issuers, and the like. It is not uncommon to characterize equity investments by capitalization ranges, or by management attributes such as "value" or "growth." Debt securities likewise can be characterized by attributes such as length of maturity and quality ratings.

STEP 5: Implement an Asset-Allocation Policy

Asset-allocation decisions are a fundamental aspect of an investment strategy and a starting point in formulating a plan of diversification. Expanding beyond the broader definition of diversification, the investment policy document should adopt the concept of asset allocation as an integral part of the prudent investment process.

STEP 6: Mutual Funds Recommendations

In order to assist in diversification and control costs, the modern investment fiduciary may consider mutual funds as a vehicle for diversification. Mutual funds offer a means of obtaining much greater diversification for what will usually be a lower cost. In addition, the plan can also achieve diversification by investing in a broad array of mutual funds.

STEP 7: Delegate Investment Management Responsibility

A trustee who meets the duties of care, skill, and caution in the selection of an investment advisor is not liable to the beneficiaries or the trust for the decisions or actions of the agent to whom the function was delegated. This is an important safeguard provided by ERISA that enables fiduciaries to shift or apportion responsibilities and associated future potential liabilities to investment professionals.

STEP 8: Investment Monitoring and Reporting

Decide on date, method, and schedule for investment reporting, monitoring, and investment manager reviews. Appropriate benchmarks must be established for review and monitoring purposes.

SECTION THREE
The Template IPS

Chapter 8

SAMPLE IPS TEMPLATES

O nce you have taken the specific actions and gathered the required material needed to assemble an IPS, any fiduciary is ready to start writing an IPS for their client. In this section we will provide two sample IPS templates that can be used as a guideline when creating, or comparing, your own documents. The verbiage, content, and descriptions of the IPS samples will clearly need to be adapted for each different client and investment scenario you have. However, by following the eight steps outlined, understanding the logic employed in each, and inserting the appropriate language, drafting an IPS will be easier and more consistent once you start using the basic framework provided.

Two Distinct IPS Samples

Two distinct IPS samples are provided. The first is intended to serve as an example of the type of information that would be included in a well-written IPS for a participant-directed 401(k) that intends to comply with ERISA Section 404(c). The second is designed for the needs of an individual investor, outside of the 401(k) or plan participant. While it is written for a high-net-worth individual setting up a family trust, similar guidelines apply to structuring an IPS for an individual in any income bracket.

Organization of Templates

Please note that each IPS is comprised of seven to eight distinct sections. At the beginning of each section are instructions and explanations of the purpose of the section, followed by examples of relevant language.

Also, each IPS format in a Word.doc file can be downloaded by financial advisors from Thornburg Investment Management's website at www.thornburg.com/IPS.

As with any legal document pertaining to your defined-contribution plan, you are advised to have legal counsel review the IPS before it is approved. This document does not comprise legal advice.

Chapter 9

SAMPLE IPS TEMPLATE #1

For a Participant-Directed 401(k) That Intends to Comply with ERISA Section 404(c)

STEP 1. Executive Summary and Background

(INSTRUCTIONS/EXPLANATIONS) *Begin by writing an overview and background of the plan. The overall objective is to have the IPS provide sufficient detail so that a third party will be able to implement the investment strategy. The IPS should be flexible enough that it can be implemented in a complex and dynamic financial environment, and yet not so detailed it requires constant revisions and updates.*

Executive Summary

Date:
Type of Plan: Defined-Contribution Plan — 401(k)
Plan Sponsor: MY CLIENT COMPANY
Plan IRS Tax Identification: 56-111111
Current Assets: $20,000,000
Participant-Directed Investment Options: Yes, 404(c) adopted
Frequency to Change Investment Options: Daily

The XYZ Company Employee Retirement Plan is a defined-contribution plan started in 1985 and is one of two qualified employee retirement plans sponsored by XYZ Company. The purpose of the XYZ Company Employee Retirement Plan is to encourage employees to build long-term careers with XYZ Company by providing eligible employees with a convenient way to save on a regular and long-term basis for retirement.

XYZ Company Employee Retirement Plan currently covers 2,500 employees. The number of employees is anticipated to increase at the rate of 5 percent per year for the next five years. Plan size is currently $20,000,000 and annual contributions should total $2,500,000-$3,000,000.

Employee contributions are made through payroll deductions each payroll period and remitted to the trustee for investment into the employee-designated investment options. The Company has elected to adopt 404(c) provisions and provides a match of $1.00 for each $2.00 contributed by the participant.

INVESTMENT OPTIONS will consist of six core equity options: large-cap growth, large-cap value, small-cap growth, small-cap blend, mid-cap blend, and large-cap blend. In addition to the six core equity-asset classes, the plan will offer a money market fund, several bond funds covering various portfolio maturity ranges, including both government and corporate bond options, plus an international equity fund and REIT fund to allow further diversification alternatives to participants.

STEP 2. Purpose of the Investment Policy Statement

(INSTRUCTIONS/EXPLANATIONS) *This section describes the purpose and intent of the IPS. Keep in mind that the IPS is not only for the use of the incumbent Committee members, but also for use by their successors to provide continuity in the management of the plan and its investments. It will also be one of the first documents reviewed in the event of a plan audit by the Department of Labor.*

This section should also clearly indicate that the plan's intent is to comply with ERISA Section 404(c) and what processes have been put in place to ensure compliance.

The purpose of this IPS is to assist the XYZ Company Employee Retirement Plan Committee ("Committee").

The Committee will discharge its responsibilities under the Plan solely in the interests of Plan participants and their beneficiaries. The Plan's investment program is defined in the various sections of this IPS by:

1. Stating in a written document the Committee's attitudes, expectations, objectives, and guidelines for the investment of all Plan assets.

2. Encouraging effective communications between the Committee and service vendors by stating the responsibilities of the Committee, the investment managers, the investment consultant, the record keepers, and administrators.

3. Establishing the number and characteristics of offered investment options.

4. Providing rate-of-return and risk characteristics for each asset class represented by various investment options.

5. Establishing procedures for selecting, monitoring, evaluating, and, if appropriate, replacing investment options.

6. Controlling and accounting for all costs of administering the plan and managing the investments.

7. Complying with all ERISA, fiduciary, prudence, and due-diligence requirements experienced investment professionals would utilize; and with all applicable laws, rules, and regulations from various local, state, federal, and international political entities that may impact the Plan assets.

Section 404(c) Compliance—This IPS has been arrived at upon consideration by the Committee of a wide range of policies and describes the prudent investment process the Committee deems appropriate. This process includes offering various asset classes and investment management styles that are expected to offer participants a sufficient level of overall diversification and total investment return over the long-term. The objectives are to comply with Department of Labor 404(c) safe-harbor provisions by:

• Notifying participants that the plan is intended to be 404(c) compliant, including a statement that fiduciaries of the plan may be relieved of certain liabilities.

- Providing participants at least three investment options that each have a different risk/return profile.

- Providing participants with sufficient information so each participant can make an informed decision about his or her selection of investment option(s).

- Permitting participants to change investment options on a [daily] [quarterly] basis. Because each plan participant shall make investment contribution and allocation decisions, the Committee shall refrain from giving what could be construed as investment advice.

STEP 3. Duties and Responsibilities

(INSTRUCTIONS/EXPLANATIONS) *Use this section to identify the parties involved with the plan investments and summarize their responsibilities. Include the retirement plan committee, investment consultant, investment manager, and custodian.*

Next, define the duties and responsibilities of all parties involved. There are numerous parties involved in the investment process and each should have his or her specific duties and requirements detailed in the IPS. This ensures continuity of the investment process so when there is a change in fiduciaries, it helps to prevent misunderstandings between parties, and helps to prevent omission of critical fiduciary functions.

XYZ Retirement Plan Committee

As fiduciaries under the XYZ Company Employee Retirement Plan, the primary responsibilities of the Committee are to:
- Prepare and maintain this IPS.
- Provide sufficient asset classes with different and distinct risk/ return profiles so each participant can prudently diversify his/ her account.
- Prudently select investment options.
- Control and account for all investment, record keeping, and administrative expenses associated with the Plan.
- Monitor and supervise all service vendors and investment options.
- Avoid prohibited transactions and conflicts of interest.

Investment Consultant

The Committee will retain an objective, third-party Consultant to assist the Committee of XYZ in managing the overall investment process. The Consultant will be responsible for guiding the Committee through a disciplined and rigorous investment process to enable the Committee to meet the fiduciary responsibilities outlined previously.

Investment Managers

The specific duties and responsibilities of each investment manager are to:

1. Manage the assets under their supervision in accordance with the guidelines and objectives outlined in their respective Service Agreements, Prospectus or Trust Agreement.

2. Exercise full investment discretion with respect to buying, managing, and selling assets held in the portfolios over which they are given authority.

3. Vote promptly all proxies and related actions in a manner consistent with the long-term interest and objectives of the Plan as described in this IPS. Each investment manager shall keep detailed records of the voting of proxies and related actions and will comply with all applicable regulatory obligations.

4. Communicate to the Committee all significant changes pertaining to the fund it manages or the firm itself. Changes in ownership, organizational structure, financial condition, and professional staff are examples of changes to the firm in which the Committee is interested.

5. Use the same care, skill, prudence, and due diligence under the circumstances then prevailing that experienced investment professionals, acting in a like capacity and fully familiar with such matters, would use in like activities for like retirement plans with like aims in accordance and compliance with ERISA and all applicable laws, rules, and regulations.

Custodian

The custodian is responsible for safekeeping of the Plan's assets. The specific duties and responsibilities of the custodian are to:

* Maintain separate accounts by legal registration.
* Routinely value the holdings.

- Collect all income and dividends owed to the Plan.
- Settle all transactions (buy-sell orders).
- Provide monthly reports that detail transactions, cash flows, securities held (and their current value and change in value of each security), and the overall portfolio, since the previous report.

STEP 4. Asset Class Guidelines

(INSTRUCTIONS/EXPLANATIONS) *This part describes the process by which asset classes to be offered to the plan participants were chosen, and it identifies the appropriate index and peer group for each asset class being offered.*

The Committee of XYZ Company Employee Retirement Plan believes long-term investment performance, in large part, is primarily a function of asset-class mix. The Committee has reviewed the long-term performance characteristics of the broad asset classes, focusing on balancing risks and rewards.

Asset Classes in Ascending Order of Risk

The following 10 asset classes were selected and ranked in ascending order of "risk" (least to most).

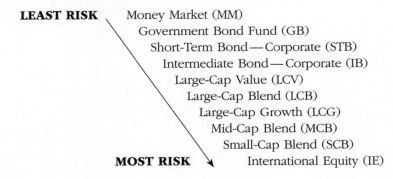

LEAST RISK   Money Market (MM)
Government Bond Fund (GB)
Short-Term Bond—Corporate (STB)
Intermediate Bond—Corporate (IB)
Large-Cap Value (LCV)
Large-Cap Blend (LCB)
Large-Cap Growth (LCG)
Mid-Cap Blend (MCB)
Small-Cap Blend (SCB)
MOST RISK   International Equity (IE)

Diversification of Asset-Class Options

The typical Morningstar™ Style analysis for core equity funds indicates that these investment options provide plan participants with an ability to diversify their portfolio holdings:

DOMESTIC EQUITY OPTIONS PER MORNINGSTAR™ STYLE ANALYSIS			
	Value	**Blend**	**Growth**
Large-Cap	Large-Cap Value (LCV)	Large-Cap Blend (LCB)	Large-Cap Growth (LCG)
Mid-Cap		Mid-Cap Blend (MCB)	
Small-Cap		Small-Cap Blend (SCB)	

In addition to the five core equity options described on the previous page, the Plan also provides money market, fixed income, and international equity investment classes to allow further diversification alternatives to the participants: money market (MM), government bond (GB), short-term bond—corporate (STB), intermediate bond—corporate (IB), and international equity (IE).

Asset-Class Index and Peer Comparisons

Asset-Class Index and Peer Comparisons for each of the ten asset classes selected for offering, the corresponding index and peer groups are as follows:

ASSET-CLASS INDEX AND PEER COMPARISONS		
Asset Class	**Index**	**Peer Group**
Large-Cap Equity		
Blend	S&P 500	Large-Cap Blend
Growth	Russell 200 Growth	Large-Cap Growth
Value	Russell 200 Value	Large-Cap Value
Mid-Cap Equity	S&P 400	Mid-Cap Blend
Small-Cap Equity	Russell 2000	Small-Cap Blend
International Equity	MSCI EAFE	Foreign Stock
Fixed Income Government Bond		
Short-Term Bond Intermediate-Term Bond	Lehman Brothers Gov't/ Credit Intermediate	Intermediate-Term Bond
Money Market	90-Day T-Bill	Money Market Database

Other Considerations

The Committee has considered the following asset classes for inclusion in the asset mix, but has decided *not* to include these asset classes at the present time: global fixed income, real estate, and high-yield bonds.

STEP 5. Investment Manager Selection

(INSTRUCTIONS/EXPLANATIONS) *This part outlines the considerations and guidelines to be employed in the selection of each investment manager or mutual fund. Your goal is to decide on the number of investment managers, choose which asset classes will be managed by each manager, and to define performance criteria and objectives. Identify the appropriate index against which each money manager will be evaluated. The one decision that is typically more difficult to make than which manager or asset-class fund to hire, is when it is time to replace the manager or fund (Part 6). When performance criteria are agreed upon in advance, the decision is easier to manage and to implement.*

The Committee will apply the following due-diligence criteria in selecting each money manager or mutual fund.

1. **Regulatory oversight:** Each investment manager should be a regulated bank, an insurance company, a mutual fund organization (Registered Investment Company), or a registered investment adviser.

2. **Correlation to style or peer group:** The investment management product (whether a fund or segregated account) should be highly correlated to the determined asset class. *(This is a critical part of the analysis since most of the remaining due diligence involves comparison of the manager to the appropriate peer group.)*

3. **Performance relative to a peer group:** The product's performance should be evaluated against the peer group's median manager return, for one-, three-, and five-year cumulative periods.

4. **Performance relative to assumed risk:** The product's risk-adjusted performance (alpha and/or Sharpe Ratio) should be evaluated against the peer group's median manager's risk-adjusted performance.

5. **Minimum track record:** The product's inception date should be greater than three years.

6. **Assets under management:** The product or manager should have at least $75 million under management.

7. **Holdings consistent with style:** The screened product should have no more than 20 percent of the portfolio invested in "unrelated" asset-class securities. For example, a large-cap growth product should not hold more than 20 percent in cash, fixed income, and/or international securities.

8. **Expense ratios/fees:** The product's fees should not be in the bottom quartile (most expensive) of their peer group.

9. **Stability of the organization:** There should be no perceived organizational problems; the same portfolio management team should have been in place for at least two years.

STEP 6. Monitoring the Investment Managers

(INSTRUCTIONS/EXPLANATIONS) *This part sets forth the process and timing of investment monitoring by plan fiduciaries. It includes required reporting by the investment managers and the schedule for performance review. In addition, it outlines considerations and guidelines to be employed when replacing the plan's mutual fund/ investment managers.*

The Committee acknowledges fluctuating rates of return characterize the securities markets, particularly during short-term time periods. Recognizing that short-term fluctuations may cause variations in performance, the Committee intends to evaluate manager performance from a long-term perspective.

The Committee is aware that ongoing review and analysis of the investment managers is just as important as the due diligence implemented during the manager selection process. The performance of the investment managers will be monitored on an ongoing basis and it is at the Committee's discretion to take corrective action by replacing a manager if they deem it appropriate at any time.

On a timely basis, but not less than quarterly, the Committee will meet to review whether each manager continues to conform to the search criteria outlined in the previous section, specifically:

1. The manager's adherence to the Plan's investment guidelines.
2. Material changes in the manager's organization, investment philosophy and/or personnel.
3. Any legal, SEC, and/or other regulatory agency proceedings affecting the manager.

The Committee has determined it is in the best interest of the Plan's participants that performance objectives be established for each investment manager.

Manager performance will be evaluated in terms of an appropriate market index (e.g., the S&P 500 stock index for large-cap domestic equity manager) and the relevant peer group (e.g., the large-cap growth mutual fund universe for a large-cap growth mutual fund) as described in the previous Section 4 of the IPS.

Watchlist Process

A manager may be placed on a *Watchlist* and a thorough *review* and *analysis* of the investment manager may be conducted when:

1. A manager performs below median for his/her peer group over a one-, three-, and/or five-year cumulative period.
2. A manager's three-year risk adjusted return (alpha and/or Sharpe) falls below the peer group's median risk adjusted return.
3. There is a change in the professionals managing the portfolio.
4. There is a significant decrease in the product's assets.
5. There is an indication the manager is deviating from his/her stated style and/or strategy.
6. There is an increase in the product's fees and expenses.
7. Any extraordinary event occurs that may interfere with the manager's ability to fulfill his/her role in the future.

A manager evaluation may include the following steps:

1. A letter to the manager asking for an analysis of his/her underperformance.
2. An analysis of recent transactions, holdings, and portfolio characteristics to determine the cause for underperformance or to check for a change in style.

3. A meeting with the manager, which may be conducted on-site, to gain insight into organizational changes and any changes in strategy or discipline.

The decision to retain or terminate a manager cannot be made by a formula. It is the Committee's confidence in the manager's ability to perform in the future that ultimately determines the retention of a manager.

STEP 7. Controlling and Accounting for Investment Expenses

(INSTRUCTIONS/EXPLANATIONS) *A key requirement of ERISA is controlling and accounting for investment expenses. In order for the fiduciary to fulfill the general fiduciary obligation to manage investment decisions with the requisite level of care, skill, and prudence, and the specific obligation of the fiduciary to defray only reasonable and necessary expenses, the fiduciary must establish procedures for controlling and accounting for investment expenses. The fiduciary is also responsible for determining if the expenses can be paid by the plan, and if the expenses are reasonable for the services being provided.*

Investment management costs and expenses fall into four categories:

1. Money-manager fees and/or the annual expenses of mutual funds.
2. Trading costs, including commission charges and execution expenses.
3. Custodial charges, including custodial fees, transaction charges, and cash management fees.
4. Consulting and administrative costs and fees.

The IPS should contain instructions and procedures on how these fees and expenses will be accounted for and monitored.

At least annually, the committee will review all costs associated with the management of the Plan's investment program, including:

• Expense ratios of each investment option against the appropriate peer group.
• Custody fees: The holding of assets, collection of income, and disbursement of payments.

- Whether the manager is demonstrating attention to "best execution" in trading securities.
- Administrative fees: Costs to administer the Plan, including record keeping, account settlement (participant balance with that of fund), allocation of assets and earnings, and (when applicable) the proper use of 12b-1 fees to offset these fees.

STEP 8. Investment Policy Review and Monitoring

(INSTRUCTIONS/EXPLANATIONS) *On an annual basis, the IPS should be reviewed to determine whether there have been any material changes to the goals and objectives or to the risk/return profile.*

The Committee will review this IPS at least annually to determine whether stated investment objectives are still relevant and the continued feasibility of achieving the objectives. It is not anticipated that the IPS will change frequently. In particular, short-term changes in the financial markets should not require adjustments to the IPS.

Prepared: .   Approved:

_____   _____
Consultant/Advisor   Committee
Date   Date

Chapter 10

SAMPLE IPS TEMPLATE #2
For a High-Net-Worth
Individual Setting Up a
Family Trust

Following is another example of an Investment Policy Statement. Although similar in nature to the prior IPS, this statement is designed for the needs of a high-net-worth individual investor, rather than a plan participant. As noted previously, the IPS is universally applicable to every type of fiduciary position—both for ERISA purposes, as well as for the management of everything from high-net-worth individuals to family trusts, foundations, endowments and eleemosynary funds.

While ERISA covers the defined contribution/benefit market, the Uniform Prudent Investors Act (UPIA) governs private trusts and eleemosynary funds. An (IPS) can be used in a variety of situations by advisors, even though it may focus on ERISA. The following variation can be used for an Individual Family Trust.

Executive Summary

*Name*_____The Jones Family Trust_____

Name of family trustees: _____

Table of Contents
Investment Policy Statement

PART I — Purpose

The purpose of the Investment Policy Statement is to provide written and formal financial goals and financial objectives.

PART II — Investment Management Objectives
Defines the nature of the relationship of how the financial advisor and individual (plan sponsor or company) will work together: how each party will manage the investment process; define levels of acceptable risk; and expected time frame and rate of returns objectives.

PART III — Roles and Responsibilities
This section defines who is responsible for what function.

PART IV — Selection of Investments and Managers
This part outlines the considerations and guidelines to be employed in the selection of investment products (mutual funds) and investment managers. This part also outlines considerations and guidelines to be employed when replacing the plan's investments and investment managers.

Part V — Investment Monitoring/Rebalancing and Reporting
This part sets forth the process and timing of investment monitoring by plan fiduciaries. It includes the required reporting by the investment managers and the schedule for performance review.

Part VI — Manager Termination
This part of the statement of investment objectives outlines considerations and guidelines to be employed when replacing the plan's investments and investment managers.

Part VII — Additional Provisions (optional)
This section addresses unrestricted investment options, company stock, participant education, communication, and anything outside of advisor management assets.

PART I—Purpose

The Statement of Investment Objectives is to assist *The Jones Family Trust* and its Investment Advisor (Advisor) in effectively supervising, monitoring, and evaluating the investment of the Trust's Portfolio (Portfolio). Its purpose is to describe formally how investment decisions are related to a plan's goals and objectives, as well as the trustee's strategic vision for investment.

It should detail an investment structure for managing *The Jones Family Trust* Portfolio. This structure includes various asset classes, investment management styles, asset allocation, and acceptable ranges that, in total, are expected to produce an appropriate level of overall diversification and total investment return over the investment time horizon.

PART II—Investment Management Objectives

The document defines the nature of the relationship of how the Financial Advisor and individual money managers will work together to manage the investment process going forward.

The Jones Family Trust desires to maximize returns within prudent levels of risk and to meet the following stated investment objectives:

(List tangible financial objectives) _____

_____

_____

_____

The Jones Family Trust recognizes and acknowledges some risk must be assumed in order to achieve long-term investment objectives, and that there are uncertainties and complexities associated with investment markets.

Establish the Expected Time Horizon

The minimum expected investment period must be at least five years for any portfolio containing equity securities. For any portfolio with less than a five-year time horizon, the portfolio should be comprised predominantly of fixed investments. This five-year minimum investment period is critical. The investment process must be viewed as a long-term plan for achieving the desired results.

Minimum Expected Investment Period: _____

PART III — Roles and Responsibilities

Investment Advisor (name and address of advisor goes here)

The Jones Family Trust has retained an objective, third-party Advisor to assist the trustees in managing the investments. The Advisor will be responsible for guiding the trustees through a disciplined investment process. The six primary responsibilities of the Advisor are to:

1. Prepare and maintain this statement of investment objectives.
2. Provide risk/return profile.
3. Prudently select investment options.
4. Avoid prohibited transactions and conflicts of interest.
5. Monitor and supervise all service vendors and investment options.
6. Control and account for all investment expenses.

Investment Managers

Investment managers are responsible for making investment decisions (security selection and price decisions). The five specific duties and responsibilities of each investment manager are to:

1. Manage the assets under their supervision in accordance with the guidelines and objectives outlined in their respective *Jones Family Trust* Agreement.
2. Vote promptly all proxies and related actions in a manner consistent with the long-term interest and objectives of the trust. Each investment manager shall keep detailed records of the voting of proxies and related actions and will comply with all applicable regulatory obligations.
3. Communicate to the trustees all significant changes pertaining to the fund it manages or the firm itself.
4. Effect all transactions for the Portfolio subject to "best price and execution." If a manager utilizes brokerage from the Portfolio

assets to effect "soft dollar" transactions, detailed records will be kept and communicated to the trustees.

5. Use the same care, skill, prudence, and due diligence under the circumstances then prevailing that experienced investment professionals, acting in a like capacity, and fully familiar with such matters, would use in like activities for like Portfolios, with like aims, in accordance and compliance with the Uniform Prudent Investor Act and all applicable laws, rules, and regulations.

Custodian

Custodians are responsible for the safekeeping of *The Jones Family Trust* Portfolio's assets. The five specific duties and responsibilities of the custodian are to:

1. Provide monthly reports that detail transactions, cash flows, securities held and their current value, and change in value of each security, and the overall portfolio since the previous report.
2. Maintain separate accounts by legal registration.
3. Value the holdings.
4. Collect all income and dividends owed to the Portfolio.
5. Settle all transactions (buy-sell orders) initiated by the Investment Manager.

Part IV — Investment Manager Selection

The Advisor will apply the following due-diligence criteria in selecting each money manager or mutual fund:

- *Expense ratios/fees:* The product's fees should not be in the bottom quartile (most expensive) of their peer group.
- *Stability of the organization:* There should be no perceived organizational problems — the same portfolio management team should be in place for at least two years.

Performance Objectives

The trustees of *The Jones Family Trust* are aware the ongoing review and analysis of the investment managers is just as important as the due diligence implemented during the manager selection process. The performance of the investment managers will be monitored on an ongoing basis, and it is at the trustee's discretion to take corrective action by replacing a manager if they deem it appropriate at any time.

On a timely basis, but not less than quarterly, *The Jones Family Trust* Advisor will meet with the trustees to review whether each manager continues to conform to the search criteria outlined in the previous section; specifically:

- The manager's adherence to the Portfolio's investment guidelines.
- Material changes in the manager's organization, investment philosophy, and/or personnel.
- Any legal, SEC, and/or other regulatory agency proceedings affecting the manager.

The Advisor has determined it is in the best interest of *The Jones Family Trust* that performance objectives be established for each investment manager. Manager performance will be evaluated in terms of an appropriate market index (e.g., the S&P 500 stock index for large-cap domestic equity manager) and the relevant peer group (e.g. the large-cap growth mutual fund universe for a large-cap growth mutual fund).

Asset Class	Index
Large-Cap Equity	
Blend	S&P 500
Growth	Russell 200 Growth
Value	Russell 200 Value
Mid-Cap Equity	S&P 400
Small-Cap Equity	Russell 2000
International Equity	MSCI EAFE
Fixed Income	
Government Bond Intermediate-Term Bond	Lehman Brothers Gov't/Credit Intermediate
Money Market	90-Day T-Bills

Measuring Costs

The Advisor will review with the trustees, at least annually, all costs associated with the management of the Portfolio's investment program, including:

1. Expense ratios of each investment option against the appropriate peer group.
2. Custody fees: The holding of the assets, collection of the income, and disbursement of payments.
3. "Best execution"—whether the manager is demonstrating attention to this in trading securities.

PART V — Investment Monitoring and Review

Advisor's Responsibilities to Gather Information and Report to Investment Committee Monthly

1. Current holdings of *The Jones Family Trust* consistent with the money manager's investment strategy.
2. Asset mix within guidelines, particularly the cash component of an equity manager's portfolio.
3. Trading costs and custodial transactions.
4. Compare performance against relevant industry indexes.
5. Evidence that the money managers are seeking "best execution" and abiding by soft dollar guidelines.

Advisor's Responsibilities to Gather Information and Report to Investment Committee Quarterly

1. Determine if there are anticipated withdrawals over the forthcoming quarter and ensure that there is adequate cash to meet disbursements. If securities have to be liquidated to raise cash, determine which money managers should be notified.
2. Review the market values of all securities held in the portfolio, especially those with limited marketability. If the money manager is providing the market values, conduct periodic audits of the valuations to ensure accuracy.

3. Review the portfolio for compliance with investment guidelines, particularly asset mix and securities guidelines. If rebalancing is required, consider the impact that forthcoming contributions and withdrawals will have on the asset mix.

4. Compute *The Jones Family Trust* total portfolio rate of return:
   • By asset class.
   • By style of strategy.
   • On a composite basis.

5. Compare each manager's results against an appropriate benchmark, and against a performance universe of the manager's style or peer group.

Advisor's Responsibilities to Gather Information and Report to Investment Committee Annually

1. Review the manager's proxy voting policy and result/issues.

2. Review the manager's brokerage and trading activities:
   • Clearing arrangements and brokerage firms utilized.
   • Quality of the trade execution.
   • Portfolio turnover.
   • Commission costs.

3. Review the money manager's organizational structure to determine if significant changes have occurred in corporate or capital structure, investment style, brokerage affiliation or practices, investment process, and professional staff.

Monitoring the Custodian

Custodial or brokerage statements should be reviewed at least annually to verify:

• That expenses are as specified, and determined in accordance with the custodial or brokerage agreement.

• Cash-management procedures are examined to verify that sweeps and other appropriate accounting methodologies are utilized.

• The custody or brokerage statements are examined to determine credits, execution, brokerage costs, and uses of commission dollars.

Part VI — Manager Termination

This part of the statement of investment objectives outlines considerations and guidelines to be employed when replacing the plan's investments and investment managers.

Potential Termination Factors

- Organizational breakdown.
- Change in personnel, ownership, or strategic emphasis.
- Inability to manage growth in assets.
- Investment process breakdown.
- Change in investment process.
- Failure to implement process diligently.
- Unexplained poor performance.

Part VII — Additional Provisions (optional)

This part may address topics such as unrestricted investment options, company stock, participant education, communication, and anything outside of advisor management assets.

NOTE: Both templates can be downloaded directly from the website at: www.thornburg.com/IPS.

Conclusion

MESSAGE TO PLAN SPONSORS

I hope this compact guide has given you a clearer understanding of three key points:

1. The definition of a fiduciary.
2. The responsibilities and liabilities that are associated with being a fiduciary.
3. The critical need for developing an IPS.

While the development and monitoring of an IPS should not be an overwhelmingly complex process, some fiduciaries may not feel comfortable trying to tackle the task by themselves. A sign of a thoughtful fiduciary is the ability to do an honest, critical assessment of the skills and time they have to devote to their responsibilities.

REMEMBER: The role of the fiduciary for a 401(k) plan is to manage the process!

Remember, ERISA encourages fiduciaries to hire prudent experts to help them execute the investment process that includes developing an IPS. Once you understand where you need help, hire the necessary experts to assist you. There are many very experienced financial advisors who specialize in providing advisory services for defined-contribution 401(k) plans. Whether you prepare the IPS by yourself or have an experienced retirement advisor assist you . . . ***Do Not Procrastinate. Do It Now!***

Glossary

The following chart breaks down the type of fiduciary accounts or entities to help organize and understand how legislation and oversight are overlaid.

	Corporate Retirement (Defined Contribution and Benefit)	Public Retirement (Defined Contribution and Benefit)	Taft-Hartley (Defined Contribution and Benefit)	Foundation/ Endowment/ Eleemosynary	Individual/ Private Trust
Legislation	ERISA	MPERS	ERISA	UPIA	UPIA
Oversight	DOL, IRS, PBGC	State Attorney General	DOL, IRS	State Attorney General	State Attorney General

401(k) plan

A defined-contribution plan that permits employees to have a portion of their salary deducted from their paycheck and contributed to an account. Federal (and sometimes state) taxes on the employee contributions and investment earnings are deferred until the participant receives a distribution from the plan (typically at retirement). Employers may also make contributions to a participant's account.

404(c)

Known as the "safe harbor" clause, this section of the ERISA regulations limit the liability of the Plan fiduciaries for the results of the participant's exercise of control by:

- Notifying participants that a 404(c) plan is constituted, including a statement that fiduciaries of the plan may be relieved of certain liabilities.
- Providing participants at least three investment options that each have a different risk/return profile.
- Providing participants with sufficient information so the participant can make an informed decision about his or her selection of investment option(s).

- Permitting participants to change investment options on a daily [quarterly] basis. Because each plan participant shall make investment contribution and allocation decisions, the Committee shall refrain from giving what could be construed as investment advice.

Allocation
The employer's contribution to a defined-contribution plan.

Asset class
A category of various types of investments. Examples of various asset classes include (there are others) the following:
Cash/money market
Bonds
U.S. large-growth companies
S&P 500
U.S. large-value funds
U.S. small-growth companies
U.S. small-value companies
International large companies
International small companies

Cash profit-sharing plan
A type of profit-sharing plan in which the company makes contributions directly to employees in cash or stock. (This type of profit-sharing plan is not a qualified retirement plan.)

Deferred profit-sharing plan
A type of qualified retirement plan in which the company makes contributions to individual participant accounts.

Defined-benefit plan
A retirement plan in which the sponsoring company provides a certain guaranteed benefit to participants based on a predetermined formula.

Defined-contribution plan
An employer-sponsored plan in which contributions are made to individual participant accounts, and the final benefit consists solely of assets (including investment returns) that have accumulated in these individual accounts. Depending on the type of defined-contribution plan, contributions may be made either by the company, the participant, or both.

Department of Labor (DOL)

The U.S. Department of Labor (DOL) deals with issues related to the American workforce — including topics concerning pension and benefit plans. Through its branch agency the Pension and Welfare Benefits Administration, the DOL is responsible for administering the provisions of Title I of ERISA.

Disclosure

Plan sponsors must provide plan participants access to certain types of information, including the summary plan descriptions, summary of material modifications, and summary annual reports.

ERISA

An acronym for Employee Retirement Income Security Act of 1974 (ERISA). Among its statutes, ERISA calls for proper plan reporting and disclosure to participants.

ESOP (employee stock ownership plan)

A qualified defined-contribution plan in which plan assets are invested primarily or exclusively in the securities of the sponsoring employer.

Fiduciary

A person with the authority to make decisions regarding a plan's assets or important administrative matters. Fiduciaries are required under ERISA to make decisions based solely on the best interests of plan participants.

Fiduciary insurance

Insurance that protects plan fiduciaries in the event that they are found liable for a breach of fiduciary responsibility.

KSOP

A plan arrangement that includes both 401(k) contributions and an ESOP.

Material modification

A change in the terms of the plan that may affect plan participants, or other changes in a summary plan document (SPD).

Median market cap

An indicator of the size of companies in which a fund invests.

Money-market fund

A mutual fund seeking to generate income for participants through investments in short-term securities.

Money-purchase plan

A type of defined-contribution plan in which the employer's contributions are determined by a specific formula, usually as a percentage of pay. Contributions are not dependent on company profits.

Multiemployer plan

A pension plan to which more than one employer contributes, and which is maintained according to collective bargaining agreements.

Mutual fund

An account with a broad range of investment options, each of which are diversified, reducing the risk to the participant.

Named fiduciary

The plan document must name one or more fiduciaries, giving them the authority to control and manage the operation of the plan. The named fiduciary must also be identified as a fiduciary by a procedure specified in the plan document.

Nonqualified deferred-compensation plan

A plan subject to tax, in which the assets of certain employees (usually highly compensated employees) are deferred. These funds may be reached by an employer's creditors.

Party-in-interest

Those who are a party-in-interest to a plan include: the employer; the directors, officers, employees, or owners of the employer; any employee organization whose members are plan participants; plan fiduciaries; and plan service providers.

Pension and Welfare Benefits Administration (PWBA)

This branch of the Department of Labor protects the pensions, health plans, and other employee benefits of American workers. The PWBA enforces Title I of ERISA, which contains rules for reporting and disclosure, vesting, participation, funding, and fiduciary conduct.

Pension Benefit Guaranty Corporation (PBGC)

A federal agency established by Title IV of ERISA for the insurance of defined-benefit pension plans. The PBGC provides payment of pension benefits if a plan terminates and is unable to cover all required benefits.

Plan administrator

The individual, group or corporation named in the plan document as responsible for day-to-day operations. The plan sponsor is generally the plan administrator if no other entity is named.

Plan participant

Person who has an account in the plan and any beneficiaries who may be eligible to receive an account balance.

Plan Document

Every 401(k) has a plan document of how it operates. The law says so. It's very detailed and contains legal information about your 401(k). In fact, the *plan* in *plan document* is why 401(k)s are called 401(k) *plans*. The law also requires that a summary of the plan document be provided to employees—this is the summary plan description.

Plan sponsor

The entity responsible for establishing and maintaining the plan.

Plan year

The calendar, policy, or fiscal year for which plan records are maintained.

Prohibited transaction

Activities regarding treatment of plan assets by fiduciaries that are prohibited by ERISA. This includes transactions with a party-in-interest, such as sale, exchange, lease, or loan of plan securities or other properties. Any treatment of plan assets by the fiduciary that is not consistent with the best interests of the plan participants is a prohibited transaction.

Profit-sharing plan

Company-sponsored plan funded only by company contributions. Company contributions may be determined by a fixed formula related to the employer's profits, or may be at the discretion of the board of directors.

Qualified plan

Any plan that qualifies for favorable tax treatment by meeting the requirements of section 401(a) of the Internal Revenue Code and by following applicable regulations. Includes 401(k) and deferred profit-sharing plans.

Risk tolerance

Risk is the variability of returns from an investment, and tolerance is leeway for variation from a standard. In other words, your capacity to tolerate unfavorable conditions during the time period you hold your investments.

Service provider

A company that provides any type of service to the plan, including managing assets, recordkeeping, providing plan education, and administering the plan.

Target-benefit plan

A type of defined-contribution plan in which company contributions are based on an actuarial valuation designed to provide a target benefit to each participant upon retirement. The plan does not guarantee that such benefit will be paid; its only obligation is to pay whatever benefit can be provided by the amount in the participant's account. It is a hybrid of a money-purchase plan and a defined-benefit plan.

Trustee

The individual, bank, or trust company having fiduciary responsibility for holding plan assets.

Uniform Prudent Investors Act (UPIA)

There are five main points of this law, which removes much of the common-law restrictions placed on investment fiduciaries. The following points are directly from the Act.

1. The standard of prudence is applied to any investment as part of the total portfolio, rather than to individual investments. In the trust setting the term "portfolio" embraces all the trust's assets.

2. The tradeoff in all investing between risk and return is identified as the fiduciary's central consideration.

3. Restrictions on types of investments have been abrogated; the trustee can invest in anything that plays an appropriate role in achieving the risk/return objectives of the trust, and that meets the other requirements of prudent investing.

4. The long-familiar requirement that fiduciaries diversify their investments has been integrated into the definition of prudent investing.

5. The much-criticized former rule-of-trust law forbidding the trustee to delegate investment and management functions has been reversed. Delegation is now permitted, subject to safeguards.

Uniform Management of Public Employee Retirement Systems Act (MPERS)

This act governs state and county retirement plans. This Act is very similar to ERISA and the UPIA in that investment decisions must be made for the sole benefit of the participants and beneficiaries of plan assets. Decisions must be made as a prudent man would make with an eye toward controlling all costs associated with the management of the assets.

Appendix

THE FIRM PROFILE

hornburg Investment Management, Inc. is a privately held investment management company based in Santa Fe, New Mexico. The firm advises the Thornburg family of mutual funds and manages separate portfolios for select institutions and individuals.

Thornburg Investment Management was founded in 1982 by Garrett Thornburg. In 1984, the firm created and offered one of the first limited-term municipal bond mutual funds in the United States, and began earning its reputation for disciplined yet consistent value investing in both fixed income and equities. Today, Thornburg Investment Management manages over $7.5 billion in mutual fund assets and separately managed portfolios.

Investment Philosophy

Thornburg Investment Management is a value investor in both stocks and bonds. Our approach to value is comprehensive, with risk control being a primary focus of everything we do. For equities and bonds, we independently value each security before reaching an investment decision. As a general rule, our bond funds are broadly diversified: We invest only in investment-grade bonds and ladder the maturities only over short and intermediate time frames. Our equity funds are focused, with a limited number of securities that we believe have compelling value.

Our investment products and services represent what we consider to be *core strategies for serious investors*. We seek to mitigate risk by consistently adhering to independent and disciplined investment strategies that over time have proven to be less volatile than those followed by other investment managers.

Six of Thornburg's funds are available for use in retirement plans, and we are an investment-only option on most 401(k) retirement platforms that utilize open architecture and provide investment choice to plan sponsors. In addition, our portfolio managers concentrate on capital preservation. The Thornburg investment discipline is conservative and fundamental, always of the highest quality, and adds value through thoughtful security selection and risk control.

About the Author

▲ ▲ ▲ ▲ ▲ ▲

ROCCO DiBRUNO, AIFA®, CIMA®, is a managing director and director of the Thornburg Retirement Group at Thornburg Investment Management. He has more than 30 years' experience working with financial advisors and plan sponsors in retirement plan sales, consulting, marketing, and product development. Rocco received his Certified Investment Management Analyst® (CIMA) designation from the Investment Management Consultants Association and his Accredited Investment Fiduciary Analyst® (AIFA) designation from the Center for Fiduciary Studies. He is also a frequent industry speaker on retirement industry trends and fiduciary governance.

This book, along with other books, is available at discounts that make it realistic to provide it as a gift to your customers, clients, and staff. For more information on these long-lasting, cost-effective premiums, please call us at 800-272-2855 or e-mail us at sales@fpbooks.com